The *Untold Story* of
HENRY *Knox*
The Man Who Saved Boston

by Danny Kravitz

Content Adviser: Major Glenn Williams
Historian
Retired U.S. Army

COMPASS POINT BOOKS
a capstone imprint

Compass Point Books are published by Capstone,
1710 Roe Crest Drive, North Mankato, Minnesota 56003
www.capstonepub.com

Editorial Credits
Jennifer Huston, editor; Heidi Thompson, designer;
Eric Gohl, media researcher; Laura Manthe, production specialist;
Kathleen Baxter, library consultant

Photo Credits
Alamy: Daniel Borzynski, 29 (bottom), INTERFOTO, 7, North Wind Picture
Archives, 29 (top), 46, Photri Images/J. Rowan, 29 (middle); Bridgeman
Images: Peter Newark Pictures/Private Collection, 54; Collection of the
Massachusetts Historical Society: 37; Corbis: Bettmann, 56; Courtesy of
Army Art Collection, U.S. Army Center of Military History: 12, 17; Flickr:
Visit Lake George, 32–33; Glow Images: SuperStock, 53; Granger, NYC: 51;
iStockphoto: wynnter, 18; Library of Congress: 21, 23, 25; Newscom: Custom
Medical Stock Photo, 11, Design Pics/George Munday, 5, Picture History, 38,
41; Wikimedia: The Athenaeum, cover, 9, NARA, 44–45, Public Domain, 8;
www.historicalimagebank.com, Painting by Don Troiani: 15; Yale University
Art Gallery: 43

Design Elements: Shutterstock

Library of Congress Cataloging-in-Publication Data
Kravitz, Danny, 1970–
  The Untold Story of Henry Knox: The Man Who Saved Boston/
by Danny Kravitz.
    pages cm.—What You Didn't Know About the American Revolution
    Includes bibliographical references and index.
    ISBN 978-0-7565-4972-5 (library binding)
    ISBN 978-0-7565-4976-3 (paperback)
    ISBN 978-0-7565-4980-0 (ebook PDF)
1. Knox, Henry, 1750–1806—Juvenile literature. 2. Boston (Mass.)—History—
Siege, 1775–1776—Juvenile literature. 3. United States—History—Revolution,
1775–1783—Artillery operations—Juvenile literature. 4. Generals—United
States—Biography—Juvenile literature. I. Title.

E207.K74K73 2015
355.0092—dc23
[B]   2014039032

Printed in the United States of America in Stevens Point, Wisconsin.
092014   008479WZS15

TABLE OF
Contents

CHAPTER *One*

It is the summer of 1775, the beginning of the Revolutionary War. For several years the British have occupied the city of Boston, Massachusetts, and most citizens who are determined to fight for American independence have fled. Under the command of General George Washington, a ragtag bunch of American colonists has surrounded the city and is trying to force out the Redcoats and prevent them from advancing any farther. The odds of regaining control of Boston from the British are hopelessly small, and the colonists are no match for the professional British Army, which has more guns and more training. The American leadership is anxious and desperate. But then one man has an idea. This is his story.

British soldiers patrolled the streets of Boston to prevent colonists from protesting British taxes and policies.

Humble Beginnings

Henry Knox was born in Boston July 25, 1750. He was one of 10 children. As a boy Henry was smart and curious so his parents enrolled him in one of Boston's finest schools. But when his father left for work in the West Indies, Henry was forced to leave school to help support his family. He was only 9 years old.

Henry's mother arranged for him to work at Wharton & Bowes booksellers in Boston, where he later became a clerk. Henry was an avid reader. He especially loved history and the stories of Greek and Roman battles. He even taught himself to read and speak French.

Although he left school at age 9, Henry Knox got an education by reading the books sold in the store where he worked.

Did You *Know?*

Henry Knox was so big and strong in his teens that he once lifted a street cart that had lost a wheel during a parade. He simply placed his shoulder under the heavy cart where the wheel had broken off, then carried it down the street. This feat showed signs of the resourceful determination that would define his accomplishments later in life.

From Bookseller to Artilleryman

As Knox's intellectual curiosities developed, his love of reading led him deeper into studies of artillery and military strategy. When Knox was 17 he joined a local military company, where he learned firsthand how to load, fire, and transport cannons. He also learned how to build trenches and fortifications to protect soldiers from enemy fire. Those skills would serve him well later in life as an artillery commander.

Knox opened his own bookstore in 1771. He stocked the store with books and magazines from London. During his free time, he continued to read and learn all he could about artillery and military strategy. He also talked to soldiers who visited the shop and became quite knowledgeable on the subject.

In 1772 Knox helped start the Boston Grenadier Corps, a militia organization formed to protect Boston from the British soldiers stationed there. He served as second in command.

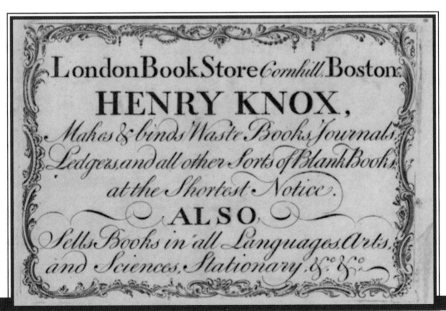

London Book Store Cornhill Boston.

HENRY KNOX,

Makes & binds Waste Books Journals,
Ledgers, and all other Sorts of Blank Books
at the Shortest Notice.

ALSO,

Sells Books in all Languages Arts,
and Sciences, Stationary &c. &c.

An advertisement for Henry Knox's bookstore

Henry Knox

By then Knox was a large man, standing 6 feet tall (183 centimeters) and weighing around 250 pounds (113 kilograms), with a booming voice and a friendly, outgoing personality. Knox was well liked and his shop was a place where many prominent Bostonians socialized, including John Adams. Adams would become an important figure in the American political movement toward independence. He later became the first vice president and then the second president of the United States.

CHAPTER *Two*

Starting a Revolution

It was a prosperous time for America, but hostility was brewing between the colonists and Great Britain over issues such as taxes. American colonists refused to pay a series of taxes to England that they believed were unfair. The Colonial assemblies were supposed to levy the taxes in their respective colonies. But with taxes such as the Stamp Act, the British Parliament imposed the tax.

The Boston Tea Party

One of the most famous events during this time was the Boston Tea Party, which was a protest against Britain's tax on tea. Disguised as American Indians, hundreds of colonists dumped 342 chests of tea into Boston Harbor on December 16, 1773. In total they dumped 46 tons (42 metric tons) of tea into the water—enough to make more than 18 million cups! That much tea would be worth nearly $2 million today.

The Boston Tea Party

Britain's King George III sent soldiers to Boston in 1768 to enforce laws, protect tax collectors, and maintain order after the passage of the Townshend Acts, a series of acts that imposed greater taxes on and authority over the colonists. But this only made the Americans angrier. Then in 1770 British soldiers killed five colonists in Boston after a protest turned violent. This event became known as the Boston Massacre.

After the Boston Tea Party in December 1773, the British closed the Port of Boston. This served to punish Bostonians by taking away their ability to trade and do business, and it only fueled the fire.

A group of militiamen between the ages of 18 and 63 was ready to take on the professional British Army at Lexington.

The collective anger of the colonists was boiling over, which ultimately led many Americans to push to become an independent nation free of England's rule.

Henry Knox would play a key role in America's fight for freedom.

An additional 4,000 troops arrived in Boston in 1774 under the leadership of General

The presence of the British in Boston and their attempt to use military force against the colonists only fueled the anger and resentment Bostonians felt. They weren't going to just let the British sail into town and take over without a fight. In response, the colonists ramped up membership in the Colonial militias.

Actual fighting between the British and the colonists began in April 1775 at Lexington and Concord, just northwest of Boston. What started out as a dispute over taxes had turned into a full-blown war. The Revolutionary War had begun.

Thomas Gage. Parliament had disbanded the Massachusetts government and sent Gage there to seize control of Boston and the surrounding areas.

The Shot Heard Round the World

As the British made their way to Concord to capture American military supplies on April 19, 1775, they encountered a small group of Colonial militiamen in Lexington. The British soldiers vastly outnumbered the militiamen 700 to 77. It is unclear who fired the first shot that day, but a small skirmish broke out. When the smoke cleared, a handful of militiamen were dead or wounded, and the British continued on their way to Concord.

While the British were searching for American weapons and military supplies in Concord, more than 2,000 militiamen descended upon the area. On a bridge just outside town, the colonists took the British by surprise and another battle erupted. As hundreds more militiamen arrived on the scene,

the British were forced to retreat. Despite this small success, the American militias were no match for the organized strength of the British Army, and they knew it.

British soldiers who were crossing Concord's North Bridge were forced to retreat when a group of Minutemen opened fire.

The War Begins for Henry Knox

Henry Knox married Lucy Flucker in June 1774. Her parents were loyalists—they sided with the British during the Revolutionary War. Lucy's father even arranged for Knox to become an officer in the British Army. But Knox declined because he was a patriot—he sided with the American Colonies during the Revolutionary War. In fact, in his bookstore's final advertisement, Knox promoted a pamphlet written by a young student and patriot named Alexander Hamilton. In the pamphlet, *A Full Vindication of the Measures of the Congress ...,* Hamilton said, "That Americans are intitled to freedom, is incontestible upon every rational principle." Posting the pamphlet clearly revealed where Knox's loyalties stood.

Meanwhile, British soldiers were arresting Bostonians who supported the revolution. Knox feared that he might be a target. When the actual fighting began, Knox knew he was no longer safe, so he and his new bride decided to sneak out of Boston. The couple donned disguises and Lucy sewed Henry's sword into her coat. They fled under cover of night, knowing that if they were caught, they could be tried as traitors and sentenced to death. They reached the docks undetected and boarded a small boat. Henry and Lucy looked back through the darkness as their vessel floated on the Charles River and the city disappeared into the horizon. Knox had abandoned his beloved bookstore, the contents of which were later stolen or destroyed. Lucy never saw her parents again.

After Henry got Lucy settled in Worcester, about 50 miles (80 kilometers) west of Boston, he headed back to join the fight. Knox enthusiastically enlisted under the command of General Artemas Ward. Armed with his military and engineering knowledge, Knox helped build fortifications around the city to contain the British. Ward was relieved that someone with Knox's military knowledge had arrived to help.

On June 17, 1775, the British Army attacked the Americans on Breed's Hill, a height overlooking Boston. At first the Americans were able to drive back the Redcoats. But eventually the Americans were forced to retreat. Although the British won the ferocious battle, which became known as the Battle of Bunker Hill, more than 1,000 British soldiers were killed or wounded compared to 440 Americans. And then someone very important arrived.

During the Battle of Bunker Hill, the militiamen were forced to fight the British in close, hand-to-hand combat when they ran out of ammunition.

CHAPTER *Three*

Henry Knox Meets George Washington

George Washington

The Continental Congress chose George Washington as commander in chief of the Continental army on June 15, 1775. Washington was on his way to Boston when he received word of the defeat at Breed's Hill.

Washington first met Henry Knox on July 5.

George Washington

George Washington was born in Virginia on February 22, 1732. As a young man, he served in the Virginia Regiment and fought on the side of the British in the French and Indian War (1754–1763). Washington represented Virginia in the Continental Congress in 1774 and 1775. Based on his reputation in the French and Indian War, Congress voted him the leader of the new Continental army in June 1775.

Washington was impressed with the fortifications Knox had supervised building in Roxbury, just southwest of Boston. He appreciated Knox's military knowledge and analytical thinking. He was also drawn to Knox's good-natured personality.

Knox was impressed with Washington and his leadership skills. The two men shared a determined nature and a strong physical presence. They quickly became friends and Knox was accepted into Washington's inner circle. He attended meetings and dinners with the general and his advisers.

Washington and his men were distressed by the situation they found themselves in. First and foremost, the Colonial soldiers were ill-equipped to fight the British. They lacked weapons,

gunpowder, skills, and money. They also lacked faith in the cause. Some discouraged troops deserted. Others headed home when their terms of enlistment expired. As a result, Washington feared that his dwindling troops would eventually be overtaken by a prolonged British attack.

Washington also worried about his army's inability to prevent the British from burning Boston to the ground. It appeared that Boston was destined to be lost or destroyed. The survival of the Continental army and America's fight for freedom were in peril.

Washington did have one small advantage, however. His troops occupied many of the heights around Boston and that put him in a position to fire down at the British. But this was of no use because the Continental army lacked a sufficient supply of cannons that they could use to rain artillery onto the British.

Henry Knox Has an Idea

Knox also understood the danger that his beloved city was in, but he had an idea. He decided to approach Washington with a plan he thought could save Boston. It was risky and daring, but if it succeeded, it could mean the difference between saving Boston or seeing it destroyed.

Back in May the Americans had seized cannons, mortars, and other weapons when taking Fort Ticonderoga, in upstate New York, from the British. Knox knew that if he could retrieve that artillery, Washington and the Continental forces could use the weapons against the British in Boston. This could save the city and drive out the British Army and Navy. The only problem was that the journey to the fort was more than 700 miles (1,127 km) round-trip. Even so, Knox approached Washington and offered to make the trip to retrieve the cannons.

Fort Ticonderoga

Fort Ticonderoga was originally built in 1755 for the French and Indian War. The British captured the fort from the French in 1759 and occupied it until May 1775. That's when Benedict Arnold and Ethan Allen and his Green Mountain Boys, a group of militiamen from Vermont, secured it for the Americans. The Americans also seized several pieces of artillery. When Knox devised his plan, those weapons were sitting at the fort unused.

In the early morning hours of May 10, 1775, Ethan Allen woke the British commander at Fort Ticonderoga and ordered him to surrender the fort.

Could It Be Done?

Whether or not he knew it at the time, Knox had volunteered for an extraordinarily difficult mission. He would have to transport the massive artillery over hundreds of miles of harsh terrain and across rivers, lakes, mountains, and valleys. Most importantly, the weather would have to work in his favor.

In addition, bringing the artillery back to Boston would require technical skill, perseverance, resourcefulness, and luck. The obstacles were so incredible that most of Washington's inner circle thought it was simply impossible.

But Knox was committed to the idea, and he was determined to save Boston. He knew the cannons were the answer to defeating the British in Boston, and he was certain that—even with the incredible challenges—he could pull it off.

Washington also realized that this plan might be the Continental army's only hope of avoiding disaster. Plus he had faith in Knox. With nothing to lose, Washington gave his permission, and Knox prepared for his mission. It was time to go get the guns.

Did You Know?

While hunting on an island in Boston Harbor in 1772, Knox lost two fingers from his left hand when his shotgun accidentally discharged. He wrapped up the wound and rowed back to Boston, where two doctors stitched him up. He was always self-conscious about his missing fingers, so he often covered his left hand with a handkerchief.

The Friendly Prisoner

On his journey to Fort Ticonderoga, Knox would encounter an infamous British spy. During his trip Knox had to share a one-room cabin with a British prisoner of war named John André. To keep his mission secret, Knox revealed nothing of his plans and claimed to be part of the British Army. The two men soon discovered that they had common interests, and as the evening wore on, they became friends.

In 1780 American General Benedict Arnold switched his loyalties and secretly offered to serve the British. Arnold was to work with André, who had been released in a prisoner exchange in late 1776. The two men worked together to devise a plan in which Arnold would surrender the fort at West Point to the British. André was captured as he tried to return to British lines after meeting secretly with Arnold. Arnold knew that papers André was carrying described their plot, so he fled to a British ship before the Americans could capture him.

André was sentenced to death as a spy in September 1780. Knox fondly remembered the time he spent with André, but in a sad twist of fate, Knox was one of the men that handed down André's death sentence. André was hanged October 2, 1780.

John André's captors forced him to remove his boots, which is where he was hiding secret papers from Benedict Arnold.

CHAPTER *Four*

Mission Impossible

Knox left Boston with his younger brother, William, on November 16, 1775. Washington had given him permission to spend $1,000 (about $30,000 today) on supplies and to hire people along the way to help him transport the artillery.

Knox first stopped in New York City to deliver a request from Washington to the local commander to send military supplies to Boston. However once they arrived, Knox learned that the army couldn't spare any heavy cannons, but smaller weapons and other artillery would be sent to Boston. Knox sent a letter to Washington to inform him of the news. It was now even more crucial to get the weapons from Fort Ticonderoga to Boston.

After leaving New York City on November 28, Henry and his brother traveled by horse up the Hudson River Valley toward Lake George. They sometimes covered as much as 40 miles (64 km) per day.

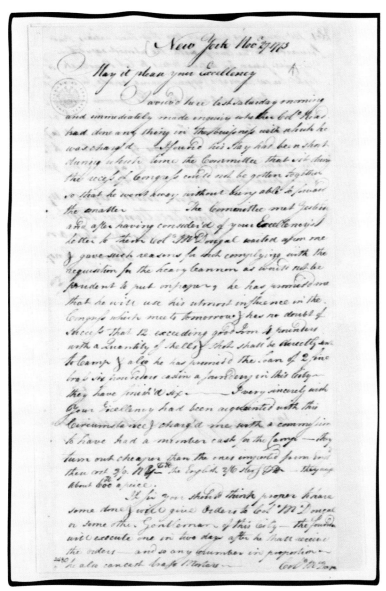

Henry Knox's November 27, 1775, letter to George Washington informed him of the artillery situation in New York City.

As the two men came upon Fort George on December 4, heavy snow started to fall. The fort was situated at the southern end of Lake George. Fort Ticonderoga, where the cannons were waiting, was near the northern end of the lake. When they arrived at Fort George, it was already mid-afternoon, so they decided to spend the night and wait out the snowstorm.

The Work Begins

After sailing up Lake George, Knox and his brother finally reached Fort Ticonderoga on December 5. There they found several pieces of artillery, including howitzers and heavy brass and iron cannons and mortars. They inspected the weapons and chose the best ones.

Among the mortars three weighed more than a ton (907 kg)

each. One huge brass cannon weighed around 2.5 tons (2.3 metric tons). This cannon was known as a 24-pounder because it fired 24-pound (10.8-kg) cannonballs. In all, the weapons Knox and his crew brought back weighed around 60 tons (54 metric tons).

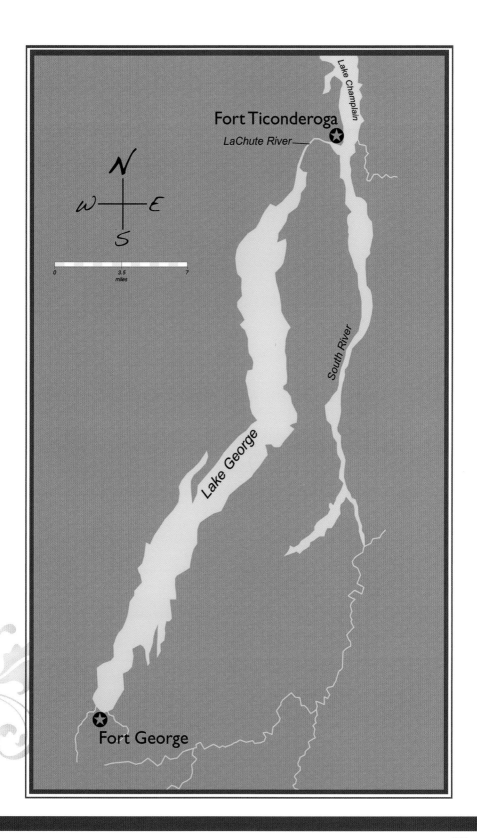

Weapons Brought Back from Fort Ticonderoga

Henry Knox sent a letter to George Washington on December 17, 1775, which included a list of the weapons he brought back from Fort Ticonderoga.

List of Weapons

8	Brass Mortars
6	Iron Mortars
13	Brass Cannons
26	Iron Cannons
2	Howitzers

Cannon, Mortar, or Howitzer?

What's the difference between a cannon, a mortar, and a howitzer?

Cannon

A cannon fires cannonballs of various weights that sail through the air and strike ships, structures, or people.

Howitzer

A howitzer fires iron shells high into the air on an arc. Those shells then explode above or near the target, showering it with fragments.

Mortar

A mortar blasts out shells at a high angle. They explode over walls or inside the target, raining fragments down upon the enemy.

With the aid of hired men and soldiers stationed at Fort Ticonderoga, Knox immediately began the work of moving the weapons. They started with the largest and heaviest pieces. Using ox carts, they transported the cannons to a nearby boat landing on Lake Champlain. Because the artillery was so heavy, it was difficult work and took longer than expected. But Knox got lucky by finding boats at the landing that were perfect for transporting the weapons.

Knox and his men sailed the weapons a short distance south down Lake Champlain then up the LaChute River. When they reached a bridge that carried Portage Road over the river, the men loaded the guns onto carts, which were driven by oxen down Portage Road to the northern end of Lake George. From there they loaded the weapons onto boats for the long journey south down Lake George. For this portion of the trip, they needed warmer temperatures because if the lake froze, their boats would be unable to cross.

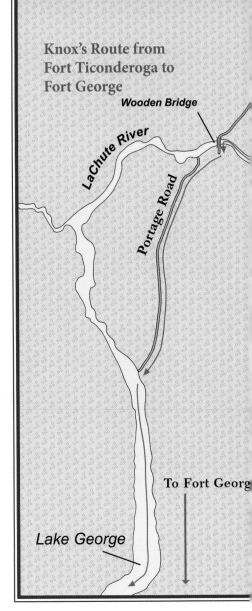

Knox's Route from Fort Ticonderoga to Fort George

Wooden Bridge

LaChute River

Portage Road

To Fort George

Lake George

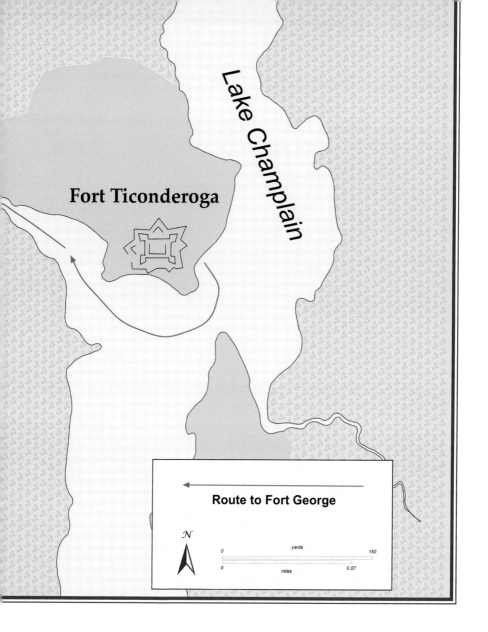

Fort Ticonderoga

Lake Champlain

Route to Fort George

$\mathcal{N}$

yards
0   150

miles
0   0.07

"It is not easy to conceive the difficulties we have had in getting them over the lake owing to the advanced Season of the Year & contrary winds—three days ago it was very uncertain whether we could have gotten them over untill next Spring."

—Letter to Washington from Knox, December 17, 1775

Within a few days, Knox and his men had removed most of the artillery from Fort Ticonderoga. They began their 32 mile- (51 km-) journey down Lake George on December 9. But there was a problem. Lake George had already started to freeze. Knox feared that the lake could freeze over completely before they finished transporting the weapons to the southern end. There was no time to waste.

The first hour of the trip was smooth sailing, with only a light breeze. But soon Knox and the others found themselves battling fierce winds and bitterly cold temperatures. For days they paddled against gusty winds

for hours at a time. Often they were so exhausted that they had to go ashore to rest and warm themselves. At times Knox and his crew also had to break through the ice that was quickly forming on the lake. They were battling against time.

"We warm'd ourselves sufficiently & took a Comfortable nap—laying with our feet to the fire—[A]bout half an hour before day break … we [set] out and in six hours & a quarter of excessive hard pulling against a fresh head breeze we reach'd Fort George."

—Excerpt from Henry Knox's diary, December 1775

Lake George

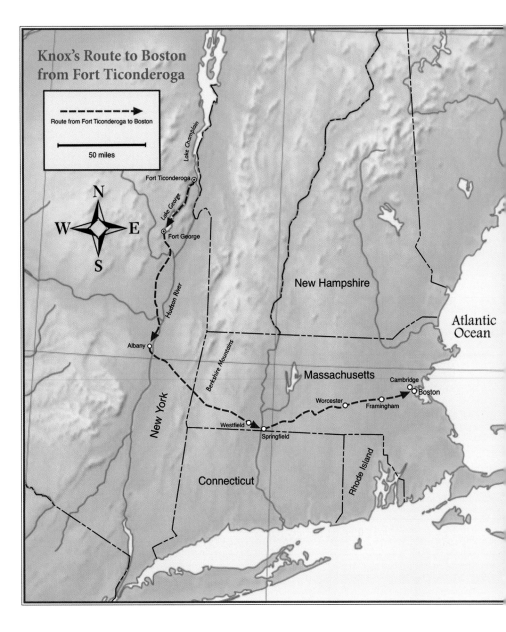

Knox's Route to Boston from Fort Ticonderoga

Route from Fort Ticonderoga to Boston

50 miles

N
W E
S

Lake Champlain

Fort Ticonderoga

Lake George

Fort George

New Hampshire

Hudson River

Atlantic Ocean

Albany

Berkshire Mountains

Massachusetts

Cambridge
Boston

Worcester
Framingham

New York

Westfield
Springfield

Connecticut

Rhode Island

The boat carrying Knox came ashore at the southern end of the lake around midday on December 11. While waiting for the other boats to arrive, Knox began planning for the next leg of the journey. They would move the guns across land through New York, following the Hudson River to Albany and then head east,

over the Berkshire Mountains in Massachusetts, eventually arriving in Boston. For this part of the trip, Knox and his men would need sleds to slide the artillery over the rough terrain. Oxen would be needed to pull the carts and sleds. And once again, the weather would have to cooperate. This time they needed snow and colder temperatures to drag the sleds across the wilderness, mountains, and valleys. They would also need rivers to be frozen solid when the sleds attempted to cross them. Weapons as heavy as the ones they were transporting could easily cause all but the thickest layers of ice to crack. And they would have to cross the Hudson River four times as they made their way back to Boston.

"I have made forty two exceeding[ly] strong sleds & have provided eighty yoke of Oxen to drag them as far as Springfield where I shall get fresh Cattle to carry them to Camp … I hope in 16 or 17 days to be able to present to your Excellency a Noble train of Artillery, the Inventory of which I've inclos'd."

—Letter to Washington from Knox, December 17, 1775

A New Problem

Knox had secured 42 sleds and oxen teams to pull them, but by December 13, he was still waiting for the other two vessels to arrive. Then he got word that the boat carrying his brother William had struck a rock and sank.

Miraculously no one was seriously injured, and the men were able to recover the boat and get it sailing again. To Henry's great relief, the other boats finally arrived on December 15.

In the end the trip down Lake George took nearly a week to complete. The lake did not freeze completely while they were crossing it, and all three boats and their cargo made it safely across.

Knox and his men loaded the artillery onto sleds at Fort George then waited for the much-needed snow. But no snow arrived. Days passed as they hoped for a change in the weather. Without snow they simply couldn't start the next leg of the journey.

"... Receiv'd advice that on the morning of the 10th the Scow had gotten from off the rock on which she had run & with great difficulty had reach'd Sabbath day point—& on the same Night the wind being exceeding[ly] high the sea had beat in her in such a manner that she had sunk."

—Excerpt from Henry Knox's diary, December 1775

A page from Henry Knox's diary from December 1775, during his journey to Fort Ticonderoga and back

King George III

Meanwhile, Back in Boston

By the end of the year, more British troops had arrived in Boston. In late October Britain's King George had made a speech before Parliament in which he referred to the rebellious Americans as traitors. Washington and his army also received a copy of the speech. The king's harsh message spoke loud and clear. The British would not stand for what was happening in America. It was evident that unless the colonists backed down, this would not be a short war.

Because the king's speech rejected any hope of reconciliation, the purpose of the war changed. No longer were the Americans simply seeking greater liberty within the British empire. They wanted to be a fully independent nation, entirely free of British rule.

To add to Washington's woes, on New Year's Day, many of his troops simply left. Their commitment to serve in the Continental army had ended, and they wanted to go home. Although new troops arrived, many of the departing soldiers walked off with the army's muskets!

"I have acted with the same temper; anxious to prevent … a state of war; still hoping that my people in America would have discerned the traitorous views of their leaders, and have been convinced, that to be a subject of Great Britain … is to be the freest member of any civil society in the known world."

—Britain's King George III in a speech to Parliament, October 27, 1775

CHAPTER *Five*

Heading Back to Boston

Henry Knox knew that every day that went by placed the American cause in more danger. Finally on December 25, a blizzard blanketed the area. This Christmas miracle dropped 2 feet (61 cm) of glistening white snow. At last the men were able to start the next leg of their journey. With the help of oxen, the sleds carrying the artillery trudged across the fresh, heavy snow toward Albany.

It was an incredible sight to see so many cannons being pulled along by oxen. "Our cavalcade was quite imposing," wrote 12-year-old John Becker, who accompanied his father whom Knox had hired as a driver. But the deep snow made their progress slow—too slow.

Despite the deep snowdrifts, Knox set off ahead of the pack so he could get to Albany to make preparations. He also wanted to deal with any problems his train of artillery might encounter on its journey. But the snow was too deep and heavy to navigate quickly.

Knox's men struggled up and down hills as they moved the artillery through the snow.

Soon the cold and snow were more than he could handle. After his horses gave out, Knox walked for miles through the deep snow. He was so exhausted that he slowed down and nearly froze to death. But when his men sent him more horses and a sleigh, he recovered and rode on.

When Knox finally got to Albany, he encountered yet another problem. The temperature had risen and the ice covering the Hudson River wasn't thick enough to hold the weight of his sleds. To thicken it Knox had men cut holes in the ice so that water would come up, freeze, and add more layers. They also poured buckets of water on the ice in an attempt to thicken it.

By January 5, all of the men and weapons had arrived in Albany. Soon temperatures began dropping. Once again the weather was working in Knox's favor.

With Knox and his men hoping the ice would hold the weight of the heavy artillery, the sleds began to cross the Hudson on January 7. It was frightening yet exciting.

"The first of the Cannon arrived here on Wednesday & the whole is on Its Way, but detained by the Weakness of the Ice in Hudsons River, occasioned by the uncommon Mildness of the Weather for several Days past, one frosty Night if not deferred too long will however put Every Thing in Order, & I hope You will soon have the Pleasure of seei<ng> all at Cambridge."

—Letter to George Washington, dated January 5–7, 1776, from Major General Philip Schuyler, who was stationed at Albany

Major General Philip Schuyler

The men were extremely cautious as they guided the artillery across the frozen waterway. They listened for any sounds of cracking, but the ice held. It seemed that the extra precautions taken to add layers of ice to the river had worked.

Nearly a dozen sleds crossed without any problems. But then as a massive 18-pounder weighing more than 2 tons (1.8 metric tons) made its way across the frozen river, the ice began to crack. Suddenly the shiny surface opened up a hole 14 feet (4.3 m) across,

Knox's artillery train faced one challenge after another as they crossed rivers, lakes, and mountains.

and the heavy cannon began to sink. Down it went into the water.

Knox immediately threw his men into recovery mode. With the help of men from Albany, they spent an entire day pulling the cannon up from the bottom of the river. They finally got all the artillery across to the east side of the Hudson on January 9. But they still had more than 100 miles (161 km) to go.

Knox's men were ready to give up after a daunting trek through the mountains.

Crossing the Berkshires

Knox had gotten the snow and cold when he needed it, but the mountains and valleys ahead presented new challenges. With steep hills and narrow valleys, the Berkshire Mountains were almost impossible to traverse, especially with such a caravan. It was more difficult than Knox had imagined.

Mile after mile the men and oxen pulled the sleds up the steep slopes. On the way down, they used ropes and chains to keep the heavily loaded sleds from sliding out of control and tumbling downhill.

After a difficult 12-mile (19-km) trek through the Berkshires, Knox's men were completely exhausted and were ready to give up. They were unwilling to continue the dangerous work and refused to go any farther.

Knox had to stop and urge them to keep going. For three hours he begged and pleaded until he finally convinced them to continue.

"It appear'd to me almost a miracle that people with heavy loads should be able to get up & down such Hills as Are here ... At Blanford [the men] refused going any further, on account that there was no snow beyond five or six miles further in which space there was the tremendous Glasgow or Westfield Mountain to go down. But after about three hours persuasion ... they agreed to go."

—Excerpt from Henry Knox's diary, January 11, 1776

Boston in Sight

As Knox and his men forged on through the rugged terrain, news spread to the colonists in the area that an artillery train was headed to Boston to help defeat the British. When they reached Westfield, residents came out to encourage Knox and his companions, bringing them food, whiskey, and cider along the way. While they were there, Knox had a 24-pounder loaded and fired to the cheers of the crowd.

After they passed Springfield, Massachusetts, the terrain smoothed out. At that point Knox traded the oxen for horses, which could move much faster.

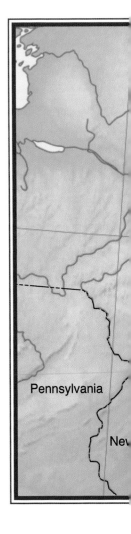

Pennsylvania

New

Did You Know?

Even after successfully transporting the artillery from Fort Ticonderoga, Knox still felt that more guns were needed. When he returned to Boston, he was happy to hear that while he was away, the American ship *Lee* captured the British ship *Nancy*. In doing so the Americans aquired 7,000 cannonballs, 10,500 flints, 2,000 muskets, and assorted musket balls.

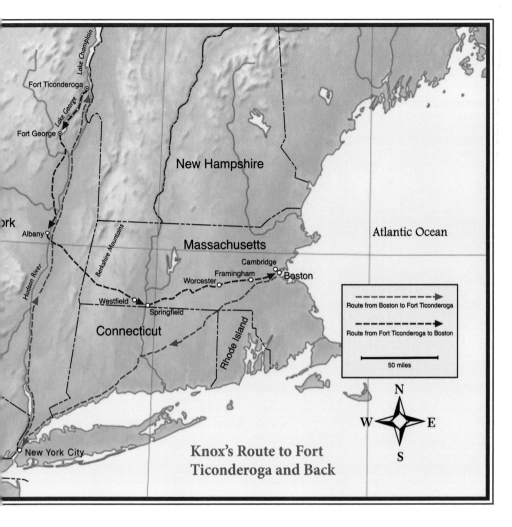

Knox's Route to Fort Ticonderoga and Back

The crew's morale improved as success started to seem within reach. It appeared they were going to make it after all.

Knox rode ahead on horseback to deliver the news of his success to Washington, who was stationed in Cambridge, just outside Boston. Finally, on January 25, the weapons rolled into Framingham, about 20 miles (32 km) from Boston. Despite all the struggles Knox and his men encountered along the way, they made it, and every piece of artillery had arrived from Fort Ticonderoga intact.

CHAPTER *Six*

Driving the British Out of Boston

Henry Knox had accomplished a truly amazing feat. When he met up with Washington in Cambridge, the commander was so impressed that he put Knox in charge of artillery for the entire Continental army. But there was still one more phase to their plan. They needed to give the British the surprise of a lifetime.

Setting Up the Guns

Washington ordered the weapons set up at locations around Boston, including Cambridge on the north side and Roxbury and Dorchester on the south side. To do this without alerting the British was an elaborate and enormous task that took weeks to pull off. Finally in early March, the Americans fired on the British for two nights. This was done primarily to divert the attention of the British away from what was happening at Dorchester.

On the third night, Washington ordered Knox and his troops to set up the rest of the artillery on the heights around Dorchester, overlooking Boston Harbor, where several British ships were docked.

The Continental soldiers worked through the night putting the cannons in place and building fortifications to hold off a British counterattack. Washington even had his troops paint logs to look like cannons to trick the British into thinking that the Americans had even more artillery than they actually did.

Under cover of darkness, American troops set up the weapons Knox had brought to Boston from Fort Ticonderoga.

When the Redcoats awoke on the morning of March 5 and saw the guns pointing down on them, they were shocked. British General William Howe is said to have exclaimed, "My God! these fellows have done more work in one night than I could make my army do in three months."

Upon seeing the influx of firepower the Americans had acquired seemingly overnight, the British became desperate. They had to come up with a solution, or they could very well lose Boston. Suddenly the tide had turned in the Americans' favor.

Howe ordered his troops to begin firing their cannons. But their guns could not reach the patriots' positions up in the hills of Dorchester. So Howe decided to attack the Americans with a ground assault. It was a desperate move that risked enormous British casualties since the Americans had fortified their positions. But

Washington kept an eye on the Redcoats as his men fortified the area around Dorchester.

Howe felt he had no other choice. Although he had been outsmarted, he was unwilling to lose Boston.

Despite knowing that he might fail, he nonetheless ordered an attack.

British General Howe ordered his troops to leave Boston in March 1776. After 11 months, the siege of Boston was over.

The British Navy was also in range of the Continental army's newly enhanced supply of firepower. British ships and soldiers were at risk of being hit by cannon fire. Then, just as the additional British troops began coming ashore on large transport ships, Mother Nature intervened once again by whipping up a

Ironically, the weather saved many British lives. It also allowed Howe to change his mind and call off the attack. He had to accept the fact that he'd been beaten.

Washington received a letter from Howe on March 8 stating that if the British were allowed to leave without being attacked, they would not destroy the city. Washington never formally answered the letter, but when the British began evacuating Boston on March 17, 1776, he allowed their exit without firing upon them. The siege of Boston was over.

terrible storm. Howling winds, torrential rain, hail, sleet, and snow completely disrupted Howe's plans. The general's desperate attack was not meant to be.

Henry Knox's Legacy

Hundreds of men had been involved in transporting the artillery from Fort Ticonderoga to Boston. But it was the determination of one man that ensured the mission's success. By delivering on his promise to do what others thought impossible, Henry Knox prevented the destruction of one of America's most important cities. Because of him, the city of Boston had been saved.

President George Washington (left) and the members of his Cabinet. From left to right: Henry Knox, secretary of war; Alexander Hamilton, secretary of the treasury; Thomas Jefferson, secretary of state; and Edmund Randolph, attorney general.

After the British left Boston, they regrouped and attacked the Americans in New York City. Henry Knox was by Washington's side through many of those battles. He was even there during Washington's famous crossing of the Delaware River on Christmas night 1776.

Knox became a major general in the army in 1782, and by the end of the war, he was a senior officer—the second in command behind Washington. In the new U.S. government, Knox became secretary of war in 1785, a position he held until 1794.

There are many famous heroes that shaped the history of the United States, seemingly ordinary people who did extraordinary things in extraordinary times.

The people who fought for America's independence were extremely courageous. When necessity challenged their abilities, a sense of duty and patriotism urged them to carry on.

Although some of the most important people of those times are lesser known, they are no less deserving of praise. Henry Knox is one of those people. His heroic success in transporting weapons from Fort Ticonderoga echoes across time. His adventure is commemorated by a series of plaques along the Henry Knox Trail in Massachusetts and New York.

July 25, 1750: Henry Knox is born in Boston.

1765–1774: England passes a series of acts, including the Stamp Act, the Quartering Act, the Intolerable Acts, and the Townshend Acts. All impose greater taxes on and authority over the colonists. The colonists protest the acts.

October 1768: British troops arrive in Boston to deal with the colonists' protests and protect British tax collectors.

March 5, 1770: The British kill five Americans during the Boston Massacre.

1771: At age 21, Knox opens his own bookstore and continues his study of military science and artillery.

1772: Knox helps start the Boston Grenadier Corps, a militia organization formed to protect Boston from the British.

December 16, 1773: The Boston Tea Party occurs.

June 1774: Henry Knox marries Lucy Flucker.

October 1774: Under the leadership of General Thomas Gage, the British Army takes control of the government in Boston.

April 19, 1775: Fighting breaks out between the colonists and the British at Lexington and Concord on the outskirts of Boston. Soon after Knox escapes Boston and joins the Colonial militia.

June 15, 1775: George Washington becomes commander in chief of the newly formed Continental army.

July 3, 1775: Washington takes command of the newly formed Continental army at Cambridge, Massachusetts.

July 5, 1775: Henry Knox meets General George Washington.

November 16, 1775: Knox sets off for Fort Ticonderoga to retrieve artillery needed to fight the British.

December 1775: Knox is appointed colonel of the regiment of artillery in early December, but he is unaware of his promotion until he returns to Boston in late January.

December 4, 1775: Knox unknowingly befriends John André, a British prisoner of war, who would later be hanged as a spy.

December 5, 1775: Henry Knox and his brother, William, arrive at Fort Ticonderoga.

December 9, 1775: Knox and his men leave Fort Ticonderoga with several dozen pieces of artillery in tow.

January 7–9, 1776: Knox leads his men in transporting the heavy artillery across the frozen Hudson River.

January 25, 1776: Knox and his men arrive outside Boston with every piece of artillery they transported from Fort Ticonderoga intact.

March 5, 1776: Washington's army surprises the British with a new influx of artillery set up on the heights overlooking Boston Harbor.

March 17, 1776: With no other choice, British troops begin their evacuation from Boston.

1782: Henry Knox is promoted to major general in the army. By the end of the war, he is a senior officer—second in command behind George Washington.

1785–1794: Knox serves as secretary of war.

October 25, 1806: Henry Knox dies in Maine at age 56.

Glossary

artillery—large guns, such as cannons or missile launchers, that require several soldiers to load, aim, and fire

howitzer—a cannon that shoots explosive shells through the air on an arc

militia—a group of volunteer citizens organized to fight but who are not professional soldiers

Minutemen—colonists who were ready and willing to fight at a moment's notice

mortar—a short cannon that fires explosive shells high in the air

loyalist—a colonist who was loyal to Great Britain during the Revolutionary War

Parliament—the national legislature of Great Britain

patriot—a person who sided with the American Colonies during the Revolutionary War

strategy—a careful plan or method

Townshend Acts—a series of acts passed in 1767 that imposed greater taxes on and authority over the American colonists

Further Reading

Burgan, Michael. *The Split History of the American Revolution: A Perspectives Flip Book*. North Mankato, Minn.: Compass Point Books, 2013.

Krull, Kathleen. *What Was the Boston Tea Party?* New York: Grosset & Dunlap, 2013.

McClafferty, Carla Killough. *The Many Faces of George Washington: Remaking a Presidential Icon*. Minneapolis: Carolrhoda Books, 2011.

Sheinkin, Steve. *The Notorious Benedict Arnold: A True Story of Adventure, Heroism & Treachery*. New York: Roaring Brook Press, 2010.

Internet Sites

Use FactHound to find Internet sites related to this book. All of the sites on FactHound have been researched by our staff.

Here's all you do:

Visit *www.facthound.com*

Type in this code: 9780756549725

Critical Thinking Using the Common Core

1. Henry Knox has been described as the man who saved Boston. Use evidence from the text to support this claim. (Key Ideas and Details)

2. Examine the infographic on pages 28 and 29. How does it help you understand the text better? How does it help you better understand what an extraordinary mission Knox and his men completed? (Integration of Knowledge and Ideas)

Source Notes

Page 16, col. 1, line 19: Harold C. Syrett, ed. "A Full Vindication of the Measures of the Congress, &c., 15 December 1774." *The Papers of Alexander Hamilton, vol. 1, 1768–1778.* New York: Columbia University Press, 1961, pp. 45–78.

Page 31, callout quote: Philander D. Chase, ed. *The Papers of George Washington, Revolutionary War Series, vol. 2, 16 September 1775–31 December 1775.* Charlottesville: University Press of Virginia, 1987, pp. 563–565.

Page 33, callout quote: "Henry Knox diary, 20 November 1775–13 January 1776." *Henry Knox Papers II.* Massachusetts Historical Society. 23 Nov. 2014. http://www.masshist.org/revolution/image-viewer.php?item_ id=463&mode=transcript&img_step=11&tpc=#page11

Page 35, callout quote: *The Papers of George Washington, Revolutionary War Series, vol. 2, 16 September 1775–31 December 1775.* pp. 563–565.

Page 36, callout quote: *Henry Knox Papers II.* 23 Nov. 2014. http://www.masshist.org/revolution/image-viewer.php?item_ id=463&mode=transcript&img_step=12&tpc=#page12

Page 39, callout quote: "King George III's Address to Parliament, October 27, 1775." 25 Nov. 2014. http://memory.loc.gov/cgi-bin/ampage?collId =rbpe&fileName=rbpe14/rbpe144/1440150a/rbpe1440150a. db&recNum=0&itemLink=r?ammem/rbpe:@field(DOCID+@lit(rbpe1440150 a))%231440150a001&linkText=1

Page 40, line 13: John Becker. *The Sexagenary: or, Reminiscences of the American Revolution.* Albany, N.Y.: J. Munsell, 1866, p. 30.

Page 42, callout quote: Philander D. Chase, ed. *The Papers of George Washington, Revolutionary War Series, vol. 3, 1 January 1776–31 March 1776.* Charlottesville: University Press of Virginia, 1988, pp. 32–36.

Page 47, callout quote: *Henry Knox Papers II.* 23 Nov. 2014. http://www.masshist.org/revolution/image-viewer.php?item_ id=463&mode=transcript&img_step=25&tpc=#page25

Page 52, col. 1, line 6: David McCullough. *1776,* New York: Simon & Schuster, 2005, p. 93.

Select Bibliography

Becker, John. *The Sexagenary: or, Reminiscences of the American Revolution.* Albany, N.Y.: J. Munsell, 1866.

Chase, Philander D., ed. *The Papers of George Washington, Revolutionary War Series, vol. 2, 16 September 1775–31 December 1775.* Charlottesville: University Press of Virginia, 1987. Founders Online, National Archives. http://founders.archives. gov/?q=Project%3A%22Washington%20Papers%22%20 Author%3A%22Knox%2C%20Henry%22&s=1511311111&r=4

Chase, Philander D., ed. *The Papers of George Washington, Revolutionary War Series, vol. 3, 1 January 1776–31 March 1776.* Charlottesville: University Press of Virginia, 1988. Founders Online, National Archives. http://founders.archives.gov/documents/ Washington/03-03-02-0021

Knox, Henry. *Henry Knox Papers II.* Massachusetts Historical Society. http://www.masshist.org/revolution/image-viewer.php?item_ id=463&mode=transcript&img_step=11&tpc=#page11

Knox, Henry. "Knox's Diary During His Ticonderoga Expedition." *New England Historic and Genealogical Register,* Vol. XXX, 1876.

McCullough, David. *1776,* New York: Simon & Schuster, 2005.

Puls, Mark. *Henry Knox: Visionary General of the American Revolution,* New York: Palgrave Macmillan, 2008.

Ware, Susan, ed. *Forgotten Heroes: Inspiring American Portraits from Our Leading Historians,* New York: Free Press, 1998.

Index

About the Author

Danny Kravitz is an Emmy award-winning writer and songwriter and a professor of screenwriting at Columbia College in Chicago. He has written for TV, film, and print media. Danny combines his passion for storytelling with his love of history. He is also a sports and nature enthusiast. He resides in Chicago, Illinois.